Due

23-233-003   Printed in U.S.A.

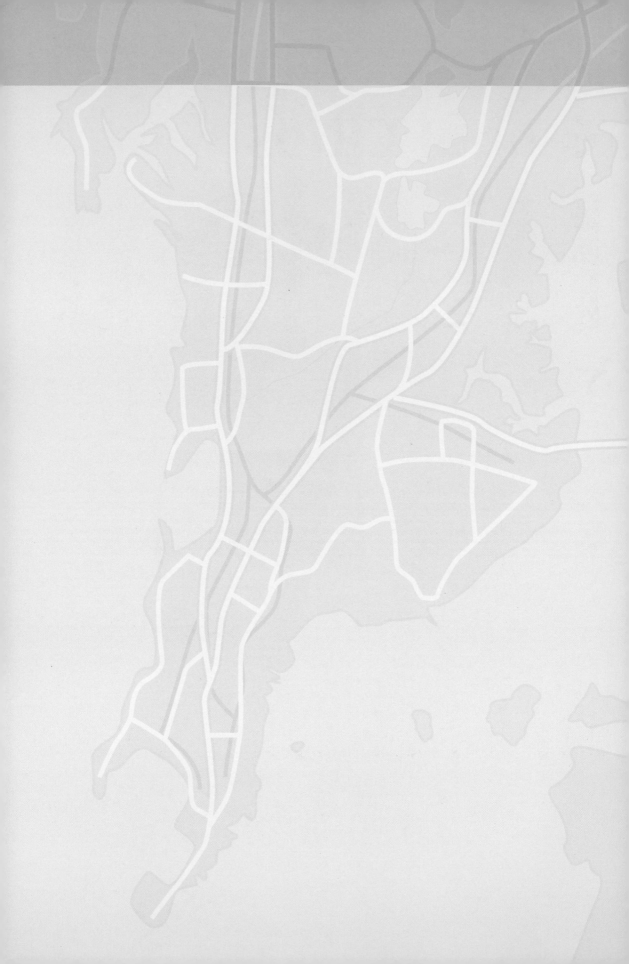

Global Cities
MUMBAI

Jen Green
photographs by Chris Fairclough

CHELSEA HOUSE
PUBLISHERS
An imprint of Infobase Publishing

Mumbai

Chelsea House
An imprint of Infobase Publishing
132 West 31st Street
New York NY 10001

Library of Congress Cataloging-in-Publication Data
Green, Jen.
  Mumbai / Jen Green ; photographs by Chris Fairclough.
    p. cm. — (Global cities)
  Includes bibliographical references and index.
  ISBN 0-7910-8851-0 (alk. paper)
  1. Bombay (India)—Juvenile literature.   I. Fairclough, Chris.   II. Title. III. Series.

DS486.B7G74 2007
954'.792—dc22   20006029173

Chelsea House books are available at special discounts when purchased in bulk quantities for businesses, associations, institutions, or sales promotions. Please call our Special Sales Department in New York at (212) 967-8800 or (800) 322-8755.

You can find Chelsea House on the World Wide Web at http://www.chelseahouse.com.
Printed in China.

10 9 8 7 6 5 4 3 2 1

Designer: Simon Walster, Big Blu Design
Maps and graphics: Martin Darlinson

All photographs are by Chris Fairclough except 13, by Bettman/Corbis; page 44, by Rob Bowden/EASI-Images.

First published by Evans Brothers Limited
2A Portman Mansions, Chiltern Street, London W1U 6NR, United Kingdom

Contents

Living in an urban world

Some time in 2007, history is made. For the first time ever, the world's population becomes more urban than rural. An estimated 3.3 billion people are now living in towns and cities. For many, it's a fairly new experience. In China, for example, the number of people living in urban areas increased from 196 million in 1980 to over 536 million in 2005.

The urban challenge...

The rapid shift to a mainly urban population is being repeated across the world and provides a complex set of challenges for the 21st century. Many challenges are local: providing clean water for the people of expanding cities, for example. Other challenges are global. The spread of diseases in tightly packed cities is a problem, as is the spread of diseases between cities linked by air routes, high-speed trains, and roads. Pollution generated by urban areas is another concern, especially because urban residents tend to generate more pollution than their rural counterparts.

▼ Mumbai and western India.

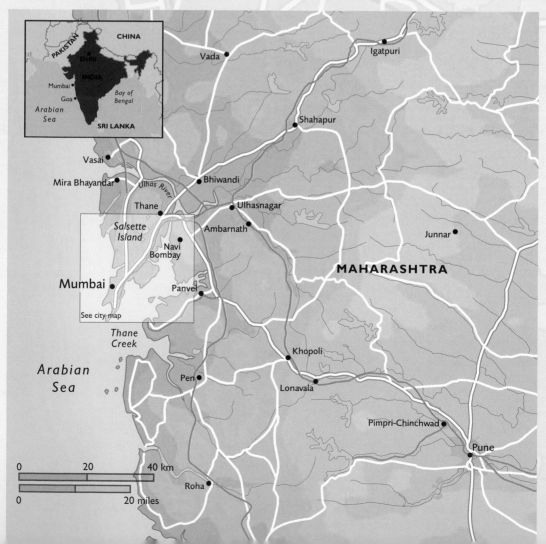

... and opportunity!

Urban centers, particularly major cities, also provide great opportunities for improving life. Cities can provide efficient forms of mass transportation, such as subway or light rail networks. Services such as garbage collection, recycling, education, and health care can all work more efficiently in a city. Cities are centers of learning and often the birthplace of new ideas. They provide a platform for arts and culture, and as their populations become more multicultural, these become increasingly global in nature.

▼ Mumbai is a densely populated city and struggles to keep pace with growth, both from within its population and from new immigrants who arrive daily.

A global city

Although all urban centers will share certain things in common, in some cities, the challenges and opportunities facing an urban world are particularly condensed. These are the world's global cities: they reflect the challenges of urbanization, of globalization, of citizenship, and of sustainable development that face us all. Mumbai is one such city. Located on India's west coast, Mumbai is India's most globalized city, with a booming economy and a rapidly expanding population. Since the 1990s Mumbai has been at the forefront of India's drive to attract foreign and domestic investment, and its commercial sector has boomed. Yet between a third and half of all its citizens live in poverty. This book introduces you to Mumbai and its people, and explores what makes Mumbai a truly global city.

India's largest city

Mumbai (formerly known as Bombay; see page 17) is the most populous city in India, with a population of around 18.3 million in 2005. Mumbai is not India's capital—that is Delhi—but it is the state capital of Maharashtra in central India. Located on a deep natural harbor, Mumbai is the country's foremost port and has long been a thriving center for industry and commerce. Since the early 1990s, Mumbai's economy has grown by leaps and bounds and an increasing level of international investment has greatly strengthened its global connections. Besides its economic status, Mumbai is best known for its thriving film and TV industry. Known as Bollywood, it is among one of India's most successful industries, producing more films each year than any other filmmaking center, including Hollywood.

▲ A view across the Colaba district. Its mix of residential and commercial buildings and waterside slums is typical of the diversity and inequality to be found across Mumbai.

The island city

Mumbai is located on islands and reclaimed land at the mouth of the Ulhas River. The city proper occupies the southern tip of an island just 3 miles wide and 14 miles long. Most of Mumbai's inhabitants, and also its industries, docks, and businesses, are crammed into this small area. Temples, mosques, and busy markets dot the center, which is punctuated by grassy spaces called *maidans*. To the north, the island of Salsette is mostly occupied by Greater Mumbai, but it includes a national park, officially known as Sanjay Gandhi National Park but more commonly called Borivali National Park.

Several bridges link Mumbai to the mainland, where suburbs such as Navi (New) Mumbai are rising to house the population overspill from the center of the city. Along with its new satellite towns on the mainland, the Greater Mumbai metropolitan area constitutes one of the world's largest urban areas.

Overstretched services

In 2005, Mumbai was one of the world's five most populous cities. As India's economic capital, it attracts large numbers of migrants from rural India every year. The city's rapidly rising population places a huge strain on housing, sanitation, transportation, and other aspects of urban infrastructure.

Mumbai is traditionally known for its cosmopolitan nature, and the city council has an optimistic vision to develop Mumbai on a par with cities like London and New York (see page 57). But widespread poverty and sprawling slums present a major challenge to this vision.

▼ Central Mumbai and its major roads and rail routes.

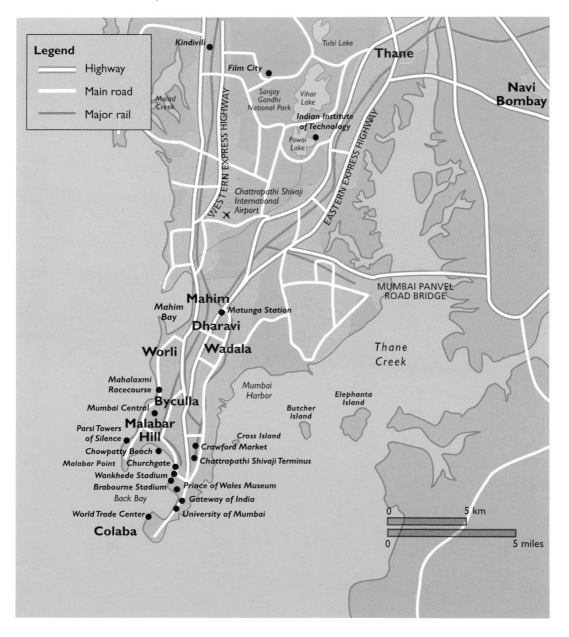

The history of Mumbai

Mumbai began as seven small islands at the mouth of the Ulhas River, home to communities of Koli people, who lived by fishing. The islands' indented coastline offered safe harbor for fishing boats, while lakes and creeks offered early settlers a plentiful supply of fresh water. This fine natural harbor formed the basis for Mumbai's growth and commerce. Since the 17th century the settlement has expanded rapidly. It now ranks as one of the world's most populous cities.

Early history

In ancient times, the area of present day Mumbai was ruled, along with much of western India, by a succession of powerful princes. These included the Buddhist emperor Ashoka in the third century B.C.E., various Hindu empires in the following centuries, and then, from the 14th century, the Muslim Mughal dynasty. In the 17th century the Marathi people from the Mumbai region, led by the famous warrior Shivaji (1627–80), challenged the Mughal rulers and eventually toppled their dynasty. Shivaji became king and founder of the Maratha kingdom in 1674. By 1750 the Marathi controlled an empire stretching across much of India, but they faced persistent rivals. Repeated raids by Afghans from the north, including a crushing defeat at the Battle of Panipat in 1761, severely curtailed their power.

▲ Tourists visit the Shiva carvings in caves on Elephanta Island. The carvings date from the eighth century.

European rule

In 1498, the Portuguese explorer Vasco da Gama made a pioneering voyage across the Indian Ocean to land on India's west coast. He returned with stories of a land rich in exotic goods and began a period of intense interest in India from the European powers of the time. Portugal became the first country to gain a foothold in India and, in 1534, secured control of the seven islands that now comprise modern Mumbai. The Portuguese named the site "Bom Bahia," meaning good bay. In 1661 Bom Bahia was transferred to the English crown as part of a wedding dowry. However, Charles II, the English king, took little interest in this distant possession and leased it in 1668 to an English trading company called the East India Company for the sum of just £10 a year.

In 1669, East India Company president Gerald Aungier visited Bom Bahia and realized it would make an excellent deep-water port. He decided to develop it by filling in the shallow waters between the islands to make one big island. Workers from neighboring Indian regions such as Gujarat carried out the work. Aungier attracted laborers, and also Indian merchants, through an offer of religious freedom, which had not been granted by either the Portuguese or Muslim rulers. The offer brought Gujarati and Goan traders, Muslim weavers, and Parsi businessmen (Parsis are followers of the Zoroastrian religion). With a flair for business, Parsis founded shipbuilding and cotton weaving industries. The population of the port, whose name had been Anglicized to Bombay, grew rapidly, swelling from around 10,000 in 1661 to 60,000 by 1675.

▼ An English merchant's home and warehouse in Mumbai in the early 18th century.

Gateway to India

By 1800, Bombay was fast surpassing Goa and Cochin to become the leading port on India's west coast. In early East India Company days, it had been isolated from the mainland, which was ruled by the Marathi, but the British defeated the Marathi in 1818 and took control of much of western India. Bombay became the gateway to India. Meanwhile major land reclamation projects increased Bombay's area to 169 square miles, just 12 square miles short of its present day extent.

Bombay's shipbuilding industry grew rapidly as the age of steamships dawned. In 1853 Asia's first railroad opened, linking Bombay with the cotton-growing lands of Gujarat and spurring the growth of the city's cotton industry. This industry blossomed during the American Civil War (1861–65), when a blockade of Confederate ports by Union forces cut off supplies of American cotton to European nations; Europe turned to India for an alternative supply. In 1869, the opening of the Suez Canal linking the Mediterranean Sea with the Indian Ocean cut journey times between India and Europe and gave Bombay added importance as a key port on the Arabian Sea. Extensive docks were built. Between 1870 and 1900 Bombay grew into a major commercial center and by 1906 the city's population had topped 1 million, making it India's second-largest city, after Calcutta (now Kolkata).

▲ The house of the first governor during the period of British colonial rule. The property is now a research institute in Parel district.

The struggle for independence

In 1857 an uprising by Indian troops against East India Company rule, known as the Indian Mutiny, led the British government to take direct control of India. This restored order, but only in the short term. By the 1880s, an increasing number of educated Indians were opposed to British rule, which exploited India's natural resources while forcing India to be a market for British manufactured goods. Bombay became a focus for this opposition and in 1885 a group of lawyers, intellectuals, and businessmen formed the Indian Congress Party with the goal of securing India's independence from Britain. From 1915 this movement was inspired and led by a lawyer named Mohandas Karamchand Gandhi (later known simply as Mahatma, or "great soul"). Gandhi developed a tactic of nonviolent resistance while working in South Africa, where he had fought for greater civil rights for the non-European population, and against racial inequalities.

Gandhi believed in India's "'self-reliance"; this was a rejection of the British policy that made India economically dependent on Britain. Gandhi spread the independence movement among ordinary Indians through campaigns such as the Salt March, in which he led a march to the coast not far from Bombay to make salt. This challenged a British monopoly on making and selling salt. Gandhi also challenged the British stranglehold on cotton goods by spinning his own cotton. His spinning wheel can still be seen in the house on Laburnum Road in South Mumbai, which was his base for 30 years and is now a museum to his life and work.

In 1942, during World War II, Gandhi and fellow Congress Party leader Jawaharlal Nehru launched the "Quit India" campaign, which called for an immediate end to British rule. Amid growing tension between the Hindu-dominated Congress Party and the Muslim League, representing Muslim interests, Britain realized it would have to give way to calls for independence.

▶ A statue to Dadbhai Naoroji in Mumbai, the first Indian member of parliament in 1892–95. He is known as "The Grand Old Man of India."

Partition

In August 1947 India finally achieved independence. Owing to irreconcilable differences between Hindu and Muslim leaders, the country was partitioned (divided) into the Hindu dominated state of India, and Muslim dominated West and East

▲ The Gateway to India, a triumphal arch built to commemorate the arrival of King George V and Queen Mary in 1911. The arch was also the departing point for the last of the British rulers. It is today Mumbai's leading landmark and tourist attraction.

▲ A young street vendor sells Indian flags for the Independence Day celebration on August 15. Mumbai played a key role in the independence movement.

international trade and commerce in India. Despite this Bombay continued to thrive, as it remained the commercial hub for of much of western India. Bombay gained further status in 1960 when it became the capital of newly formed Maharashtra state following political boundary division changes within India.

Pakistan (the latter became Bangladesh in 1971). Partition resulted in huge upheaval, as between 7 million and 12 million Hindus and Muslims migrated across the borders of the newly defined states. Many of the Hindus moving south from West Pakistan (now Pakistan) settled in Bombay.

In 1948 the last of the British administration departed India via Bombay's ceremonial archway, called the "Gateway to India." Nehru became India's first prime minister and the Congress Party remained in power until 1977. He advocated industrial and political autonomy, a policy that led India to impose heavy taxes on foreign businesses, thereby limiting

▲ The Maharashtra state parliament buildings in Mumbai. Becoming the state capital in 1960 gave the city political as well as economic significance.

Religious tensions

By the mid-1980s Bombay overtook Kolkata as India's most populous city. The city's population has grown dramatically ever since, and particularly following national free-market reforms in the early 1990s that sparked rapid economic growth. This has not been without its problems, however, including widespread poverty and rising crime and violence. Racial and religious tensions started to simmer in a city that had been renowned for tolerance. In the climate of unrest, the right wing, pro-Hindu Maharashtran party Shiv Sena rose to power in the municipal council. Shiv Sena means "Shivaji's army," referring to the 17th-century warrior. In 1992, Muslim-Hindu tensions exploded in 14 weeks of violence in Bombay, with riots and bombings that killed over 1,100 people. Since then there have been bombs and continuing low-level harassment of Muslims and "outsiders." In 1995, Shiv Sena took power from the Congress Party in the Maharashtra state elections, adding to its control of the city. One of their actions has been to rename Bombay as Mumbai, emphasizing the city's Hindu identity. The name *Mumbai* has ancient roots, being derived from Mumbadevi (a Hindu goddess) and Aai, meaning "mother."

CASE STUDY

Bhimrao Nana Jankar

Bhimrao Nana Jankar is a police sub-inspector who has been in the police service for 28 years, the last five of them with the traffic police. "As a police officer on the streets you really notice the changes in this city," he explains. "The traffic is a good example of the changes—good and bad. The new traffic lights they introduced are computerized and timed so that we no longer have to stand in the road directing traffic—that was very dangerous! But now there is simply too much traffic. The city cannot cope, and the traffic controls are breaking down. The ban on rickshaws and the new one way systems are helping, but the city is not keeping pace with change. History is moving too fast."

The people of Mumbai

The people of Mumbai are known as "Mumbaikars" and their numbers swell continually as yet more immigrants enter the city on a daily basis. These new Mumbaikars are attracted by the hope of work and a better lifestyle, but the reality is often very different. Mumbai certainly offers a good lifestyle for its growing middle class, but the majority of Mumbaikars live in poverty and in sometimes appalling conditions, far worse than those they left behind. The newer immigrants often face hostility from the existing population—many of them older immigrants.

An expanding city

The majority of Mumbai's immigrants come from rural Maharashtra, but thousands originate from other parts of India. New migrants are mostly young men who come seeking work and leave their families behind. This pattern means that Mumbai has a significant gender imbalance, with around 1.25 men for every woman. For many newcomers the only work available is in the low-paid informal sector in jobs such

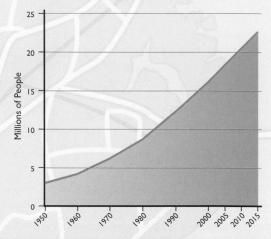

▲ Mumbai population growth 1950–2015.

▼ People come to Mumbai with the hope of a better life, but for many life can be very difficult living without basic services in the city's sprawling slums.

18

as construction, unskilled manufacturing, or collecting and selling trash (see page 51). As a result many find it hard to afford housing, a shortage of which has pushed prices very high. They end up sleeping in makeshift shelters on the streets or on vacant land such as alongside the railroad tracks. The rising population and shortage of affordable housing means that Mumbai is expanding ever outward. People who cannot afford to live in the center find places to live on the outskirts of the city and travel in each day to work. Most commuters journey by rail, spending up to four hours daily on local trains that are crammed to bursting (see page 43).

▶ With housing in desperately short supply, thousands of people are forced to construct makeshift homes alongside city roads. They live in unbelievably cramped conditions and many suffer from poor health caused by breathing vehicle exhaust fumes.

CASE STUDY

Immigrant worker

Nirwal Chaudhari is 21 and works as a casual laborer on building sites across Mumbai. "My home is in West Bengal," explains Nirwal, "on the opposite side of India. I came to Mumbai about two months ago to join my brother. There are many people from West Bengal trying to find work here. At the moment I am working on a building project to make a pedestrian underpass near one of the main railway stations in southern Mumbai. The pay is not very good and by the time I have sent some money home I cannot afford anywhere to stay so I live on the streets close by. If I had skills I could earn more money, but I didn't finish my education and I have no qualifications. I can't even read or write. There are so many people like me looking for work in Mumbai, I can't see much hope for a better job in the future. In fact things will only get worse as the city really expands over the next few years."

Greater freedoms

Most immigrants come to Mumbai for economic reasons, but some find the city attractive because it is more tolerant of India's complex caste system than elsewhere. Ancient Hindu custom assigns everyone a fixed place in a hierarchical society according to his or her caste. India's constitution of 1947 outlaws discrimination on the grounds of caste, but the system remains strong in rural areas, binding children to follow family professions and prohibiting marriage outside one's caste. In cities, and especially Mumbai, things are more relaxed and people live in ways that would be taboo in many rural villages.

▲ A Hindu priest makes offerings to the gods. Mumbai is dominated by the Hindu faith, but well known for its general religious tolerance.

Religious tolerance

When the East India Company first invited people to come and work in Mumbai they promised everyone the right to religious freedom. Mumbai retains this liberal tolerance today and Mumbaikars freely worship and follow their customs alongside people of other religions. This made the Hindu-Muslims riots of 1992–93 all the more shocking for Mumbaikars, and many have sought to improve communal harmony—although they are undermined by political and social leaders who sometimes try to inflame ideas of difference. Hindu, Muslim, Buddhist, and Christian festivals are all celebrated exuberantly, often by a wide sector of the community. In August or September, Mumbai's most famous festival, Ganesh Chaturthi, honors the elephant-headed Hindu god, Ganesh, who is the city's patron. The eleven-day festival culminates

▶ The Mahim Muslim mosque—shrine of Makhtum Fakih Ali Paru— with men praying on mats in the road at midday prayers on Friday.

in clay images and giant statues of the god being immersed in the sea by crowds wading off the town's beaches. In October or November, Divali, the Hindu festival of lights, is also celebrated enthusiastically, with firecrackers exploding everywhere and candles lit in shrines and alleyways. Lakshmi, the Hindu goddess of wealth and prosperity, is also revered in this city known for moneymaking. For Muslims one of the most important festivals is Eid ul-Fitr, which marks the end of Ramadan, the Muslim month of fasting. New clothes are worn, feasts are held, and the city's mosques throng with people coming to pray and wish each other Eid Mubarak ("blessed festival").

Many faiths

Around two thirds of Mumbaikars are Hindu, compared to around 80 percent in India as a whole. The majority of Mumbai's Hindus originate from the states of Maharashtra or Gujarat to the north. Islam

has the next largest following in Mumbai at almost a fifth of the city's population, slightly higher than the national average of 14 percent. Christianity and Buddhism compose the other major faith groups of Mumbai and there are also Parsis, Jains, Sikhs, and Jews. Jains are well known for a lifestyle that involves meditation and a great respect for all living things. This means Jains have a vegetarian diet, for example. Parsis originate from Persia (modern day Iran), but most arrived in Mumbai from neighboring Gujarat state, where they fled following the Muslim invasion of Persia in the 10th century. As followers of Zoroastrianism, Parsis do not bury or cremate their dead, but leave them to be picked apart by vultures in circular walled enclosures called Towers of Silence. In Mumbai these towers are located in the southwest of the city. Famous as entrepreneurs, Parsis have founded many of Mumbai's most successful companies, including the Tata Group, one of Mumbai's biggest businesses. It manufactures cars, trucks, and chemicals and supplies energy, information technology, and hundreds of other products and services (see page 33).

▲ Men collect holy water at Bhika Behram Parsee well in the city center close to Churchgate station.

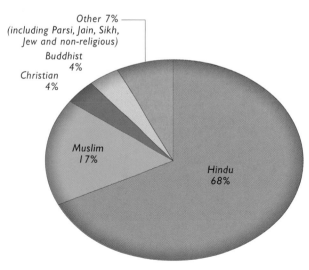

Other 7%
(including Parsi, Jain, Sikh, Jew and non-religious)

Buddhist 4%

Christian 4%

Muslim 17%

Hindu 68%

▲ Mumbai's religious makeup in 2005 (%).

Many tongues

Mumbai's historical attraction to immigrants from across India means that many languages are spoken on its streets. The most common are Hindi, Marathi—the official language of Maharashtra—and English, which is widely used as the language of business and by Mumbai's middle class. Bambaiya Hindi ("Bombay-speak"), a colloquial blend of Hindi, Marathi, and English, is commonly used to bridge language barriers. Other languages include Gujarati, Bengali, Urdu, Tamil, and Malayalam.

Population and services

In 2005 the metropolitan area of Mumbai had an average population density of 99,611 people per square mile. However, an estimated 40 percent of Mumbai's population live in less than 5 percent of its total area—meaning parts of the city, particularly around the center, are much more densely populated. For at least half of these people that means living in overcrowded slums or on the streets.

Besides the obvious shortage of housing, population pressure places considerable strain on Mumbai's infrastructure (transportation, water, electricity, and so on). Experts estimate that up to half of the city's population have insufficient water, sanitation and electricity. Electricity is provided by BrihanMumbai Electricity Supply and Transport (BEST), a government-owned body. A disastrous deal with the now-collapsed U.S. company Enron has done little to help alleviate the shortage. Power cuts are common, especially in the hot and humid summers, when air conditioning and fans work continuously in the city's offices and wealthy homes. Water comes primarily from lakes beyond the city center, including two in Borivali National Park. Current supplies leave at least 20 percent of the population without enough water. Most of these are among the poorest residents and they are left with little option but to use contaminated supplies that threaten their health, or find the money to buy water from water sellers.

▲ People line up to collect water from a standpipe in the slum district of West Colaba. Providing basic needs such as clean water is a major problem in Mumbai.

Prosperity and poverty

Mumbaikars represent all economic groups, from the fabulously wealthy to the desperately poor. The city is renowned for its well-educated middle class, many of whom work in the city's rapidly expanding information sector (see page 31). With money to spend, many middle-class people enjoy an affluent lifestyle, frequenting the coffee shops and fast food outlets that have sprung up across the city, and using credit cards to buy designer clothes and electronic goods in new Western-style malls. The lifestyle and social expectations of this growing middle class are a world apart from Mumbai's poor, who may live just outside on the streets. But it is Mumbai's poor that form the majority, with around a third of Mumbaikars (some 6 million people) estimated to live on less than US$1 a day and millions more faring little better.

▲ These young women are members of Mumbai's growing middle class population, today enjoying many of the trappings of life familiar to people in other global cities such as London or New York. Here they catch up in one of Mumbai's many new coffee shops.

Living in the city

Mumbai's downtown area is located at the southern tip of the island, curled around the sweeping curve of Back Bay. The docks and business quarter lie to the east, with wealthy Malabar Hill to the west, and bazaars (markets) and slums sandwiched in between. Across these different districts are many different styles of life, with varying access to basic services such as water, sanitation, health care, and education. In fact, few cities in the world can rival Mumbai for such enormous inequalities in living standards.

Varied housing

Mumbai's housing varies between extremes of wealth and poverty. Fashionable districts such as Malabar Hill (see page 11) contain the luxury homes of film stars and business leaders. At the other end of the scale are sprawling slums and makeshift street shelters. North of Matunga Station lies Dharavi, often referred to as Asia's largest slum. Built over a marsh, the slum is home to 1 million, packed into an area of just 0.67 square miles. Narrow, winding tracks separate tiny homes that house more than a dozen people. Furniture is scarce in these two-story dwellings partly because floor space is needed for sleeping and working.

▲ The slum district of Dharavi has grown up around the edge of a marsh on wasteland through which the main water pipes feeding the city pass. It has some of the worst living conditions in the city.

In slums such as Dharavi, and Bhuleshwar in the center, the very poorest residents live in makeshift dwellings cobbled together from scraps of salvaged wood, corrugated iron and plastic. Electricity and water supplies, if present at all, are severely overstretched and

▲ These apartment buildings in Powai district are air conditioned, with modern shops, restaurants, and other services.

sanitation is poor. In some slum pockets over 100 people share a single toilet; in others there are no toilets at all. In 2005, it was estimated that the city held some 3,000 of these slum pockets, housing a total of 6.8 million people—roughly equivalent to the population of London. Incredibly, despite these difficult conditions, a shack in this area might cost $10,000. Few new migrants to the city can afford to pay that much money, and so they sleep on the streets. It is thought that at least 27,000 families were living on streets with no shelter at all in 2005. These are not just transient populations—some "pavement dwellers" have lived in the same patch for years.

▲ A young woman and her baby earn their money begging from tourists and business people in downtown Mumbai. They have no home and live on the city streets day and night.

Slum clearance

In 2004–05, the city council pursued a policy of slum clearance in an effort to "clean up" Mumbai's streets. The Municipal Corporation of Greater Mumbai (MCGM) launched a drive to demolish slums built since 2000. In spring 2005 some 9,000 makeshift dwellings were bulldozed, but there were no plans to relocate or re-house the occupants or to offer them compensation for their lost homes. Slum activists condemned the MCGM for its inhumane actions and pressed the authorities to provide for the dispossessed, but nothing was done. Most people simply added to overcrowding elsewhere by moving to yet another slum area in the city.

Education

Primary schooling in India is free and compulsory, but not secondary schooling. MCGM-run schools, called public schools, provide 10 years of primary and secondary education in over 10 languages. In practice, poor children have little chance of completing their education unless they win one of the few available scholarships. Many leave school at an early age to earn money for their families and some never attend, instead starting work alongside their parents from as young as five years old. Class sizes are large, with some 40 students per teacher. Many middle-class parents prefer to send their children to private schools, including convents and Jesuit-run schools, which have better facilities and also teach in English.

Secondary school is followed by two years at Junior College, where students specialize in arts, science, the law, or commerce. Following this they may pursue a degree course at the University of Mumbai, the Shreemati Nathibai Damodar Thackersey Indian Women's University (for female students only), or the Indian Institute of Technology (IIT). The latter is one of the most prestigious universities in India and IIT graduates are highly sought after in the job market. Mumbai owes part of its recent economic success to the growing numbers of well-educated, English-speaking graduates that its institutions produce. Such skills are increasingly important in a more global economy based on information technology and communications.

▲ This classroom is in a private middle class school for girls, close to the city center. Those who can afford it often choose to privately educate their children due to overcrowding and a lack of resources in many state schools.

Health care

Mumbai's wealthier residents enjoy an excellent standard of health care provided by world-class private hospitals. Municipal hospitals and clinics run by the state or nongovernmental organizations (NGOs) provide other health care options, but there is little provision for free or low-cost care for the poor. In all, Mumbai has over 1,000 health centers and 40,000 hospital beds, but these facilities are woefully inadequate to cope with the city's vast population. Doctors and other medical staff are often reluctant to work at state-run clinics and hospitals because of the low pay offered there.

▲ A nurse at the Colaba district government clinic reminds mothers waiting to immunize their children to keep their medical cards safe.

CASE STUDY

Health and the poor

Neera Aykar and Pradnali Judhav are health workers in one of the many clinics operated by NGOs for the less affluent people of Mumbai. The clinic is in Colaba, close to one of Mumbai's major slum districts. "Many of the health problems in Mumbai are linked to poverty," explains Neera, "such as cholera and typhoid, which are caused by poor access to water and sanitation. Respiratory illnesses linked to the air pollution are also common." The clinic Neera and Pradnali work for provides checkups, vaccinations, and consultations for those who can't afford them. They also provide education about basic hygiene, child care, nutrition, and family planning. "Today is one of our twice-yearly polio days," says Pradnali. "Parents or relatives will bring their young children here to be immunized against polio, one of the diseases we are at last getting on top of. Mothers and fathers are really motivated to get their babies immunized against the childhood problems that we suffer in India. We are seeing over 300 children every day!"

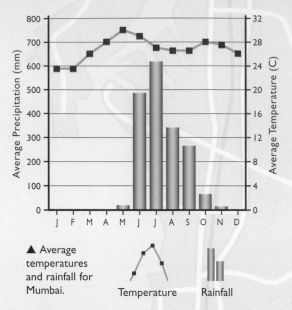

▲ Average temperatures and rainfall for Mumbai.

Temperature   Rainfall

▲ Up to 10,000 men work in the famous Dhobi Ghats, taking in laundry from all over the city. Their day begins at dawn before the full heat of the day.

Climate

Mumbai has a tropical climate, and being coastal is also influenced by maritime (sea-related) conditions. There are two main seasons: a rainy season (the monsoon) running from March to October, and a dry season from November to February. The monsoon brings torrential rain as it moves northward across India from the Indian Ocean. Mumbai receives up to 75 inches of rain at this time, most of its yearly average. On July 26, 2005, a record 37 inches of rain fell in a single day—and in that year extremely heavy monsoon rains caused extensive flooding and the loss of at least 400 lives (see page 52). Temperatures in Mumbai range from 54°F to 100°F. April to June are uncomfortably hot and humid, with temperatures regularly soaring into the 90s. Temperatures are lower in the dry season, especially during January and February, when cool breezes blow in off the ocean.

The working day

In Mumbai the city streets are rarely quiet; people are constantly coming and going about their daily business. In some districts, work starts very early in the morning, such as in the laundry district—the Dhobi

Ghats. From 4:00 a.m. the *dhobi-wallahs*, or laundrymen (*wallah* roughly translates as "worker"), begin scrubbing and pounding dirty laundry in small walled enclosures connected by water channels. Shortly after, trains begin disgorging the commuters who make the daily journey from the suburbs. Morning streets are thronged with traffic and pedestrians on their way to work.

▼ Many office workers, like these below, depend on street vendors for their lunches, showing the link between the formal and informal sector.

At lunchtime, many workers grab a snack from one of Mumbai's myriad fast-food sellers. Other workers enjoy a hot lunch cooked at home that is ferried in from the suburbs courtesy of the *dhaba-wallahs*—Mumbai's famous hot lunch delivery service. When the working day ends, people may hurry home or linger to watch a game of cricket being played on one of the city's *maidans* (open spaces).

▶ During rush hour the city streets teem with people, here around the main bus station in the center of Mumbai.

CASE STUDY

The *dhaba-wallahs* of Mumbai

Shankar Kadam is one of Mumbai's famous *dhaba-wallahs*, who deliver hot lunches from homes in the suburbs directly to over 100,000 office workers every working day. Each morning suburban households prepare a lunch (typically rice, lentil daal, and curried vegetables), which is placed in insulated lunchboxes. These are collected by a team of *dhaba-wallahs* who deliver them to the nearest railroad station for the journey to Churchgate station in the city

center. Another team of *dhaba-wallahs* meet the trains, gather the meals for their area, and deliver them to the waiting workers. Later the whole process is reversed to return the empties. This incredibly complex system rarely goes wrong, as Shankar explains: "We use a system of color coding to know where the meals belong. Many of us cannot read and write well, so the colors make it easier and are quick too. I deliver 25 meals a day using my cart. Others use bicycles or trays that they balance on their heads. My father is a *dhaba-wallah* too and I began learning from him when I was 14 years old. I have been doing this for 12 years now."

The Mumbai economy

Mumbai's economy was originally founded on its textiles industry and role as a seaport. These remain part of today's economy, but since the 1980s, industries employing skilled labor have become increasingly significant, including electronics, information technology, and a growing financial services sector. This diversity has given Mumbai the status of being India's leading industrial and commercial center. Its economy generated a third of India's tax revenue and around 40 percent of foreign trade revenue in the early 2000s.

▶ Though new industries may dominate the Mumbai economy today, the port still performs a vital function. Here, imported sand is being loaded onto trucks for use in the booming construction industry.

Economic boom

From independence in 1947 until the 1990s, global investment in Mumbai (and India more widely) was limited because unwieldy bureaucracy and heavy tariffs discouraged foreign-owned businesses. These conditions grew out of the Congress Party's belief in self-reliance and state-led economic management for India. By the late 1980s it became clear that in an increasingly global economy, such restrictions would leave India behind.

In the early 1990s the barriers to international investment were reduced by the free-market reforms of Prime Minister P. V. Narasimha Rao. Foreign investment began to flood into India, helping the Indian economy to grow by some 7 percent a year in the late 1990s. The newfound wealth caused a boom in demand for Indian goods, boosting manufacturing and retail and creating new demands in service industries such as banking. Another service industry, telecommunications, grew extremely fast during this period as industries embraced the new commercial opportunities of computers, the Internet, and e-commerce. Throughout this period, Mumbai retained and further consolidated its position as the economic heart of India. In 2006 the Indian economy grew by 7 percent, of which 5 percent came from Mumbai alone.

The service sector

Service industries today make up the largest sector of Mumbai's economy including jobs in banking, insurance, real estate (land and property sales), transportation, information technology, retail, tourism, and social services. Mumbai is India's financial capital. It is home to Asia's oldest stock exchange, the Bombay Stock Exchange, along with the Reserve Bank of India, the National Stock Exchange, and the Mint. These institutions are clustered around Dalal Street in South Mumbai, in an area

▲ The new building for the National Stock Exchange located in the new commercial district known as the Bandra Kurla Complex, or BKC for short.

▼ The Bombay Stock Exchange in the area known as India's Wall Street in southern Mumbai.

nicknamed "India's Wall Street," after the famous New York financial district. Until recently, the trading floors of Mumbai's two stock exchanges were frenetic, with dealers shouting and signaling wildly, but trading is today done via computers in remote offices.

In the early 2000s the financial sector boomed, with record highs repeatedly recorded on the stock exchange. During the same period, property prices in Mumbai rose enormously. From 2005 to 2007 prices for apartments in the center of the city rose between 30 and 50 percent.

Social services

As the capital of the Maharashtra state, Mumbai is where many employees for the state and municipal governments work, and they form a significant percentage of Mumbai's workforce. The MCGM and BEST (which provides electricity and transportation) are both major employers, with the MCGM alone having over 123,000 registered employees. State and municipal workers provide community services, transportation, utilities and many other services.

Entertainment and tourism

Entertainment is one of Mumbai's biggest industries. The film studios and production houses of Bollywood, center of the Indian film and TV industry, are located here. Mumbai's film industry originated in the 1890s and has grown into a prolific sector making an incredible 1,000 films or more every year. The industry supports other jobs in the manufacture of film equipment, the production of movie-related merchandise, and even tourism, with many studios offering visitor tours (see page 45).

Tourism makes a very significant contribution to the city's economy, with the trade being geared to both foreign visitors and Indian vacationers. Many Mumbaikars are employed in the industry, including guides with foreign language skills, travel agents, and hotel workers. Small colleges train people in tourism-related disciplines. Post-training entry-level pay in a travel agency is typically around US$40 a month, rising to US$130 a month for a company manager.

▼ Moviegoers emerge from one of the latest Bollywood films to be screened in Mumbai, the home of the film and media industry in India and one of the most important media centers in the world.

Offshore industries

Mumbai has a large number of companies in the "offshore" sector, providing services such as call centers and data processing to overseas companies at cheaper rates than in their home markets. In the early 1990s this sector performed basic tasks such as testing pharmaceuticals, writing software, and staffing call centers. In the early 2000s, the sector grew by an amazing 30 to 40 percent each year and now performs more sophisticated services for international clients, including research. Overseas companies invest in Mumbai's offshore sector because of its low labor costs and a plentiful supply of English-speaking graduates, who answer inquiries for international credit card, insurance, and transportation providers. The offshore sector is a major factor that is driving forward Mumbai's increasingly global economy.

Manufacturing

Mumbai is India's leading center for manufacturing and engineering, oil refining, and electronics. Gems and jewelry, chemicals, textiles, and processed foods are all major products. Though less important than it was 50 years ago, the textile industry still employs over 40,000 workers. The shipyards of eastern Mumbai produce vessels of all kinds, from tugs to tankers, submarines, and warships. The city's extensive docks are the busiest in India, handling 40 percent of the nation's maritime trade.

▲ Mumbai has an enormous naval dockyard where ships are both built and serviced for the Indian Navy.

Several huge Indian-owned manufacturing companies are based in Mumbai, including the Tata Group, the Godrej Group, and Reliance Industries Limited. Tata and Godrej are both family-run businesses, started in the 19th century. Reliance was founded in 1932. Together they employ hundreds of thousands of people, produce a huge range of goods and services, and export products around the world. Tata alone, among other things, produces vehicles, steel, pharmaceuticals, and packaged tea; works in information technology; and supplies central Mumbai with electricity. In 2004–05 its revenues were US$17.8 billion, 2.8 percent of India's gross domestic product (GDP). Reliance, with interests in oil and gas extraction, petrochemicals, and textiles, has annual group revenues of over US$20 billion, and Godrej has revenues of over US$1 billion.

▲ A promotional stand in a new shopping precinct advertises one of the latest products produced by Tata motors, just one division of the Tata business empire.

The informal economy

Like many cities in less economically developed countries, Mumbai has a large informal economy composed of businesses that aren't registered or regulated, with employers and employees avoiding laws, charges, and taxes. The sector includes thousands of small workshops involved in activities such as tanning and leather-working, jewelry-making, and garment manufacture. There are also a host of unskilled and semi-skilled workers such as taxi drivers, mechanics, construction workers, garbage sellers, and street hawkers. Such workers are highly visible, but in stark contrast there are tens of thousands of craft workers, called *karigars*, who toil long hours in backstreet sweatshops. This hidden workforce includes many child workers who are exploited by their employers.

Karigars involved in jewelry-making use acid and other toxic chemicals and work with acetylene torches linked to fuel canisters. Occasionally the canisters explode; in June 2000, an exploding gas cylinder in a Zaveri district workshop killed 24 workers. Many of the *karigars* in Zaveri work 12 hours at a stretch for minimal pay, often sleeping and eating on premises that may be barred and locked because of the precious metals being used. Some workshop owners base themselves in Zaveri because health and safety rules that must be observed in more regulated areas, like the industrial parks, are difficult to enforce. Despite its lack of regulation, the informal sector makes a large contribution to the city economy. Bombay University's Sociology Department estimates that the informal sector comprises 65 percent of Mumbai's workforce. Because of this the MCGM would like to formalize the sector, not least because this would increase tax revenues.

▲ An informal sector worker repairs a camshaft in his open-air workshop close to the docks area of Mumbai. The informal sector performs many such vital support roles for the more formal economy.

▲ Textile workers sewing beads onto fabric in a city sweatshop. Working for at least 12 hours a day they sit cross-legged on the floor. Workers may live and eat in the same premises they work in.

Shyama Pada Awon, jeweler

Shyama Pada Awon owns a small jewelry business in Zaveri Bazaar in Bhuleshwar, a city district known for its craft workshops. Shyama is originally from Kolkata, where he trained as an apprentice, but has worked at Zaveri for 25 years. "There are some 15,000 people producing jewelry in Zaveri," he explains, "selling it here and overseas. I make and sell jewelry to order for local customers, but also have customers in Canada, the United States, the United Kingdom, and South Africa—even here in Zaveri we are in a global market! I employ 10 artisans, also from Kolkata, who mostly work with gold and diamonds. Even though I sell my goods all over the world I would never want to live anywhere but Mumbai."

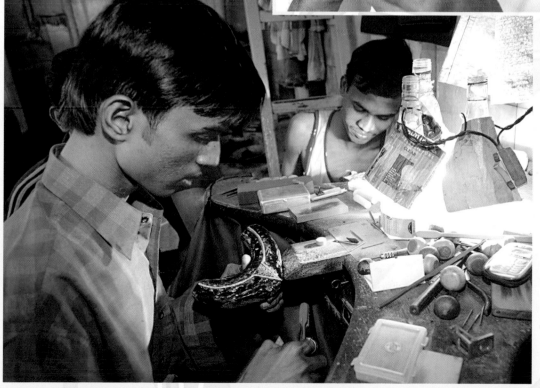

Managing Mumbai

Mumbai is the capital of Maharashtra state, which is split into 35 districts. Greater Mumbai forms two of these districts: the center of the city, often called Island City, and the suburbs of Greater Mumbai, in total an area of 169 square miles. The Municipal Corporation of Greater Mumbai (MCGM) manages these two areas—it is India's largest and wealthiest civic authority. The MCGM has an annual budget of over US$1.6 billion and employs a workforce of over 123,000 people in order to provide civic services to Mumbai's residents.

The Mayor and Municipal Commissioner

There are two main figures in the MCGM—the Mayor and the Municipal Commissioner. The Mayor's role is largely ceremonial, and includes chairing the Corporation's meetings and appearing as the public face of the city. The city's elected council members appoint the mayor for a term of two and half years.

Real power lies with the Municipal Commissioner, a state official who is appointed by the Maharashtra state government every five years. All major political parties put forward candidates for the post. The Municipal Commissioner heads the city council and has extensive executive powers, with ultimate responsibility for the city's infrastructure, including water provision, waste disposal, roads, parks, and schools. The MCGM is also responsible for the city's health, running hospitals and clinics and taking action to prevent epidemics. The fire

▼ Government buildings in Mumbai.

▲ Municipal workers repair part of the dam on Lake Vihar, one of the key water sources for Mumbai.

department, port authorities, and electricity and transportation authority are also divisions of the corporation. The council is made up of 232 members, of whom 227 are elected; the other five are appointed for their administrative expertise.

As capital of Maharashtra, Mumbai is home to the state assembly (Vidhan Sabha), the state government offices (Mantralaya), and the residences of the state Governor (the representative of the national government in Delhi) and Chief Minister.

Citizens' groups

Citizens' groups and nongovernmental organizations (NGOs) are very active in Mumbai. They include housing and slum associations and environmental pressure groups. Informal-sector unions such as the Hawkers' Union and the National Alliance of Street Vendors are also active on behalf of unregistered workers. One of the leading slum activists, Jockin Arputham of the Society for Promotion of Area Resource Centres (SPARC), began his career as an activist spearheading a campaign to pressure the MCGM to remove garbage from the slums. Action by citizen groups like these has often been successful in getting the civic authority to recognize its duties. Arputham has since won the prestigious Magsayay Award, which recognizes work by citizens. Arputham

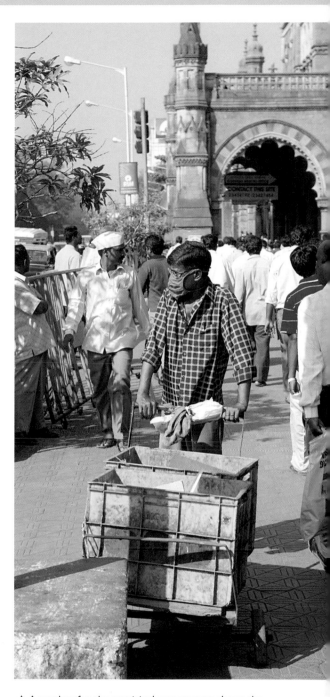

▲ A worker for the municipal government cleans the streets close to the center of the city. He wears a mask to protect himself from air pollution.

condemns the MCGM's periodic slum clearances (see page 25) and has put forward an alternative plan to house the city's homeless in vacant lots, for which low rent could be paid.

Law and order

The authority of the Bombay High Court (the name has not been changed to Mumbai) extends throughout Maharashtra and the state of Goa to the south. Mumbai's police form part of the state police. They are headed by a Commissioner and divide the city into seven policing zones. The separate traffic police divide the city into 17 traffic zones. According to the police, Mumbai has a "moderate" crime rate, with the figure of 27,527 crime incidents logged in 2003, representing a fall of 11 percent from the figures for 2001. In 2004, there were 3,247 reported car thefts, 2,969 burglaries, and 250 murders. In the first half of 2005 there were 122 murders, compared with 135 during the same period in 2004. Information technology-related crime has risen steeply since 2000. Even the authorities admit that the bribing of officials to avoid penalties for minor offenses is widespread, and no concerted or serious attempts have been made to prevent the practice. For example, motorists caught committing traffic violations report getting off without charge after offering the officer concerned a bribe.

▶ A policeman riding his motorbike through the congested Mumbai traffic.

Street hawkers

Mumbai's street hawkers are one of the city's most characteristic sights, lining the streets with makeshift stalls and carts, selling everything from food to books, clothes, kitchenware, and electrical goods.

MCGM estimates of their numbers vary widely—from 20,000 to 320,000—of which only 17,000 have official permits. Unofficial hawkers have historically been tolerated in exchange for bribes to police and local officials.

In 2001, the MCGM launched a series of clearances to remove street hawkers from around train stations on the grounds that hawkers block the free movement of traffic and pedestrians, and are unsightly. The MCGM also claims to be acting in the interests of

◀ A hawker sells tea to passersby. Across the city, street hawkers are a common sight and an important part of the local economy, providing services and goods.

local residents and shopkeepers. Stalls were bulldozed, goods seized, and some hawkers allegedly beaten. The MCGM offered some hawkers the chance to relocate to indoor "hawking plazas," but many hawkers say this would kill their business, which relies on passing trade from commuters.

Opposition to the clearances has come from the Hawkers Union, which maintains the crackdown is unfair, since the authorities are removing the stallholders' livelihood without providing alternative employment. Some local residents and shopkeepers have also opposed the clearances, because they regularly bought goods from the hawkers. Some also believe that far from being an eyesore, the hawkers added character and color to their neighborhoods.

▶ A street hawker sells clothes and fabric on a makeshift streetside stall. Such activity is typical of the informal sector in Mumbai and has been the target of controversial city clearances in some areas.

CASE STUDY

Dropada Syamrao Palchatri, street hawker

Dropada Syamrao Palchatri is a street hawker in downtown Mumbai, selling fruit and vegetables to passersby. "My day begins every morning at around 5:00 a.m.," explains Dropada, "when I go to buy my produce from Crawford Market. It then takes me around three hours to get to my spot here in Colaba and I am normally ready to sell by 9:00 a.m. I have been using this same spot for 29 years! I don't have a license—you can only get one of those if you know the right people in the city authorities. With no license the police are always a problem, and I often have to pay a bribe to carry on my business."

Transportation for Mumbai

Mumbai has an extensive transportation network, both within the city and connecting to national and international destinations. But some forms of public transportation, notably the trains, are in poor repair, with massive overcrowding a major problem. All the city's transportation networks are heavily congested and unable to cope with a rapidly growing population and economy. The MCGM is widely criticized for spending large sums on projects such as road overpasses, which encourage the use of private cars and taxis by the better off, but only a pittance on maintaining public transportation that is used by millions every day.

▲ Heavy road traffic along Marine Drive. Congestion is becoming a major problem for Mumbai because higher incomes for the middle class mean greater car ownership.

Air traffic

Mumbai's airports are the busiest in India, accounting for around 30 percent of India's air passengers and 35 percent of its air cargo. Chattrapathi Shivaji International Airport (see page 11) handles international traffic, while domestic flights also pass through Santa Cruz Domestic Airport. There are calls for a new airport to be constructed at Navi Mumbai across the harbor, to ease noise and pollution caused by planes circling overhead as they wait to land at Mumbai's overused airports. The capacity at Mumbai's airports has been particularly challenged by the growth and popularity of low cost internal airlines (mainly used by business customers). In 1991–92, Chattrapathi Shivaji International Airport handled 4.2 million domestic passengers; by 2003–04 this had almost doubled to 8 million.

National railroads

Rail services date from the 1850s, with connections to all parts of India. Two major branches of the historic national Indian Railways operate from Mumbai. Central Railways, serving destinations in eastern and southern India, is based at Chattrapathi Shivaji Terminus (also known by its former name of Victoria Terminus, or VT for short). Western Railways, serving northern India, operates from Mumbai Central. Three types of rail services—passenger, express, and "superfast" trains—connect to Delhi, Kolkata (Calcutta), Chennai (Madras), and other destinations.

▶ Passengers wait for long distance trains at Chattrapathi Shivaji Railway Terminus, more commonly known by its former name, Victoria Terminus, or simply VT.

Highways

Mumbai has several fast highways, with a new expressway linking to Pune, Maharashtra's second-largest city. The construction of new highways is part of Mumbai's plans to improve its infrastructure, partly in an effort to attract more foreign business. Bus services ranging from air-conditioned coaches to crowded, dilapidated jalopies link Mumbai with cities in the neighboring states.

Sea travel

Mumbai is a natural deep-water port handling one sixth of India's seagoing trade. There are three main enclosed docks: Indira, Victoria, and Prince's Docks. There are specialized facilities for handling oil products which are located on an island,

Jawahar Dweep, in the harbor. India's economic growth and increasing global trade connections mean that traffic through Mumbai's port has increased in recent years. In 2000–01 the port handled around 30.4 million tons, but this had increased by around 28 percent to 38.8 million tons in 2004–05. Crucial to this increase in traffic has been improved port efficiency, with the average turnaround for a vessel entering the port being reduced from 4 days to 3.3 days between 2000 and 2005.

Mumbai is also an important navy base and prior to air travel was India's main arrival and departure point for international travelers. Today, the main form of passenger traffic operating from Mumbai are the vessels departing the Gateway of India for the excursion to Elephanta Island in the bay.

▲ A ship waits off the coast for a free berth to unload its cargo in Mumbai's commercial port, one of the busiest ports in the world.

Traveling in the city

Millions of commuters make the daily trek from suburbs such as Thane and Navi Mumbai to the city center—not just "white collar" office workers, but also laborers, hawkers, and artisans of all kinds. During rush hours, city roads are virtually gridlocked with every form of transportation, including cars, taxis, bicycles, scooters, buses, and rickshaws. Exhaust fumes cloud the air and the noise is deafening, with people shouting and sounding their horns. Because of congestion and a shortage of parking places, 88 percent of commuters use public transportation. Most people use trains to make longer journeys from the distant suburbs, while buses are inexpensive for short trips (as little as one rupee, or US$0.02).

▲ Motorbikes are an easy way to navigate the crowded Mumbai streets, but they are not safe—few people wear safety helmets.

Inner-city trains

The Mumbai Suburban Railway (MSR) operates one of the most heavily used urban rail systems in the world, with over 186 miles of electrified track in Greater Mumbai. The western, central, and harbor lines all link to mainland suburbs, with the eastern branch running via the docks and across the bay to Navi Mumbai. During peak travel periods it is not uncommon to find up to 5,000 passengers crammed onto nine-carriage trains designed with a capacity of just 1,710. This gives Mumbai's urban rail system the highest passenger density in the world, but such high density is also extremely dangerous. Hundreds of people are injured or die every year by falling from overcrowded trains (many have no doors). In 1999 the Ministry of Railways and the Government of Maharashtra formed the Mumbai Railway Vikas Corporation (MRVC) to

▲ Passengers at Chattrapathi Shivaji Railway Terminus. More than 2.5 million people use this station every day, on one of the world's busiest urban rail networks.

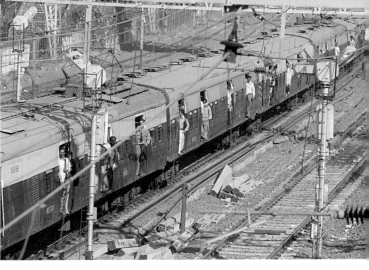

modernize the rail system and improve safety. Longer 12-carriage trains have been ordered and platform extensions are planned to help relieve congestion at stations. Rail infrastructure is also being upgraded and historical problems such as trespassing and encroachment by slum dwellers are being addressed to improve safety.

In the early evening rush hour of July 11, 2006, eight bombs went off on the Mumbai train network. Over 200 people were killed, either on commuter trains or at stations. The bombs went off without warning, causing havoc in the tightly packed trains. The police immediately shut down the entire Mumbai train network, stranding hundreds of thousands of people in the city overnight. No group claimed responsibility for the attacks, but the authorities blamed Islamic militants seeking to wrest the northern state of Kashmir from Indian control.

▲ Passengers hang out of the open doors of overcrowded commuter trains.

Buses and taxis

BrihanMumbai Electric Supply and Transport (BEST) is responsible for Mumbai's extensive bus network and operates a fleet of around 3,390 buses, including single-deckers and double-deckers that resemble the old red London buses. Some services became disabled-friendly in 2005. In the early 2000s, the BEST transportation division employed 38,000 people including drivers, conductors and administrators—11.2 employees per bus! Besides buses, black-and-yellow taxis are common for travel within downtown Mumbai, though are unaffordable to many. Beyond the city center (where they have been banned to relieve congestion) three-wheeled auto-rickshaws operate a cheaper alternative to taxis.

▼ Beyond the city center, three-wheeled auto-rickshaws (like these near Kurla station) are a popular and cheap form of transportation.

Culture, leisure, and tourism

Mumbai is a thriving center for culture and entertainment, offering a wide range of visual and performing arts to suit the cosmopolitan tastes of its citizens. As the home of Bollywood, the city has long had a major influence on the cultures of South Asia, and in recent years this influence has become increasingly global.

The media and the arts

Internationally renowned writers Salman Rushdie and V. S. Naipaul have written extensively about Mumbai and its energetic and diverse population. In *India: A Million Mutinies Now* (1990) Naipaul describes the grime, sprawl, and poverty of Mumbai. In works such as *The Moor's Last Sigh* (1995) Salman Rushdie describes the city as quintessentially Indian, the meeting and merging place for cultural influences from all parts of India. Many other writers and artists have been drawn to the city by its heaving energy.

Mumbai has two major and influential modern art galleries, Jehangir Gallery and the National Gallery of Modern Art. Mumbai's growing middle class provides an affluent new audience for a broad and thriving range of music and performance that includes folk, religious, and modern dance, and musical styles from classical to pop.

▲ Divali, the Hindu festival of light, is held every year over five days in either October or November. This stall holder is selling paper and cloth flowers to passersby on their way to the temples.

The festival year

In a city of such diverse religious and cultural attitudes, public festivals are very important. The cultural year starts with January's Banganga Festival of Music near Chowpatty Beach. In February, the Elephanta Festival of classical music and dance is held on Elephanta Island, with many of India's foremost musicians and dancers taking part. In August and September, the Hindu Ganesh Chaturthi celebrations are a major cultural event, dating from the 1890s, when nationalists promoted the festival to reassert India's cultural heritage in the face of British rule. The festival culminates in statues of the god Ganesh being immersed in the sea. A local arts and crafts festival, the Kala Ghoda, runs from November to January.

Bollywood

The film studios of Mumbai account for a high proportion of India's annual output of films and TV programs. Most films produced here are made in Hindi, and generally belong to a genre called "masala movies." The name means "spicy mixture," and is used because these films contain a little of everything—music, song, dance, romance, comedy, and action—in an involved plot in which the villain is eventually defeated and the hero wins the heroine. Bollywood's output also includes religious and historical epics, more "serious" films by directors such as the late Satyajit Ray, and movies geared to western audiences, such as *Salaam Bombay*, *Mississippi Masala*, and the major 2004 hit *Bride and Prejudice*. Mumbaikars are generally star-struck, creating a huge following for Bollywood actors such as Rishi Kapoor, Amitabh Bachchan, and Aishwarya Rai.

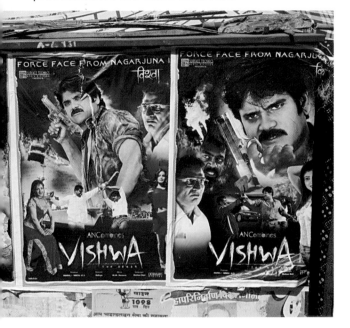

◄ Posters advertise one of the latest offerings from Mumbai's thriving film industry, known worldwide as "Bollywood."

CASE STUDY

Alhad Godbole, newspaper editor

Mumbai is India's foremost center for media and publishing. Top-selling English-language newspapers such as the *Times of India* and *India Express* are published here, while Marathi dailies such as *Loksatta* and *Maharashtra Times* are widely read. Alhad Godbole is editor of *Loksatta*, which sells 500,000 copies daily, published in four editions. Alhad says that *Loksatta* specializes in "journalism of courage."

"We do stories that other newspapers shy away from, such as about the Indian mafia or about corruption," he says. "In India people have a great thirst for the written word. There was a time when one newspaper would be handed around between five or six households; now there are many people who read five or six newspapers every day." Despite globalization and the recent boom in modern media such as the Internet and satellite television, Alhad is optimistic about the future of his industry, insisting "the print media will never die in India."

▲ Buses pass the grand facade of Chattrapathi Shivaji Railway Terminus (Victoria Terminus), one of the architectural treasures of Mumbai.

Architecture

A huge variety of architectural styles can be seen in Mumbai. Perhaps the best known are the Neo-Gothic edifices built by the British, such as Crawford Market and Chattrapathi Shivaji Terminus. The latter mixes styles that recall the architecture of Britain's industrial north with local emblems such as carved peacocks, lions, and monkeys. In 2004 Chattrapathi Shivaji Terminus was listed as a World Heritage Site. Another of Mumbai's most famous buildings is the ornate Taj Mahal Palace and Tower, a luxury hotel near the Gateway to India commissioned by the wealthy Parsi businessman J. N. Tata and opened in 1903.

Mumbai's modern architecture comprises the new gleaming skyscrapers of downtown offices and an increasing number of luxury apartments, many with their own retail and leisure facilities and even their own schools. These are built to accommodate the new affluent middle class. At the other end of the spectrum, Mumbai is famous for its chawls, large tenement buildings with central courtyards for poorer residents. Organizations like SPARC (see page 37) are active in co-designing dwellings for the very poorest, making sure that they meet the needs of people who live, sleep, and work in the same space.

▲ In confined areas a new form of street cricket—gully cricket—has emerged.

Sports

Mumbai's most popular sport, cricket, is played daily on the city's grassy spaces or *maidans*. A local variation called "gully cricket" is suited to confined spaces such as streets and gullies, with different rules, for example, for the scoring of balls reaching the boundary. The city's two stadiums, Wankhede and Brabourne, host major league cricket matches, with the national and city teams inspiring widespread and intense support. In recognition of the city's dominance of the national team, Mumbai is home to the Board for the Control of Cricket in India (BCCI). Soccer, played during the monsoon season, is the next most popular sport. There is also great interest in field hockey, although this is less popular than in the past. Mumbai continues to produce many players for the Indian national team—one of the best field hockey teams in the world.

Sports such as tennis, badminton, and squash are played at clubs throughout the city, of which the plush Bombay Gymkhana is the most famous. However sports facilities are scant for non-club members. Golf has a growing following, with the authorities giving the go-ahead to the construction of several new courses in Greater Mumbai, partly to cater to foreign businessmen. The construction of these new courses is eating away at the mangrove swamps that border the mainland of Greater Mumbai, a move that is condemned by environmentalists.

The town's beaches are popular with joggers as well as water-sports enthusiasts and people just relaxing. Horse races are held at Mahalaxmi Racecourse every Sunday during the season, which extends from November to February. Major races are glittering social occasions attended by Mumbai's rich and famous. A huge betting industry is associated with all sporting activity, and illegal bookmakers are regularly accused of conspiring to fix matches in their favor. This led to a crackdown by the authorities in May 2006, with many bookmakers fleeing the city.

▲ Polo horses training for a game at Mahalaxmi Racecourse.

Leisure time

Mumbai's hardworking executives have little time for leisure, while the poor are often too busy just getting by to take much time off. However, in a city where moneymaking is very important, some of the most popular leisure activities are free. In the evening and on weekends, people take a walk in city parks and gardens or stroll along the *maidans*, watching the world go

▲ People enjoy a leisurely walk along Juhu Beach in the early evening sunshine. Juhu is one of the most popular beaches in the city.

by. Large numbers take the air on the town's beaches, eating snacks such as *bhel puri* and *kulfi*—ice cream flavored with cardamom, saffron, and pistachio nuts. In the evening Chowpatty Beach takes on a carnival atmosphere, with ferris wheels, fortune-tellers, performing monkeys, and snake charmers. People go to theaters to catch the latest movie, while younger people meet up at the fast-food outlets that are springing up downtown. South Indian and Chinese cuisine remain very popular among Mumbaikars.

▲ A souvenir seller on Elephanta Island.

Tourism

Mumbai's role in India's tourist industry has traditionally been as an air hub, with the majority of international visitors moving on elsewhere in India within a day or two. With tourism set to become the world's largest industry by around 2020, Mumbai has woken up to the potential benefits of tourism and is striving to attract visitors from both within India, and abroad. There are now tourist offices across the city providing advice, in several languages, on hotels, restaurants, shopping, and sightseeing in Mumbai. One major initiative has been the development of studio tours in collaboration with the Bollywood studios. Visitors can watch live takes of films, tour movie sets, take part in a dance routine, or see an entertainment show.

Major attractions

The majority of international visitors to Mumbai arrive between September and April, when cooler and drier weather means the climate is less oppressive. This period coincides with some of Mumbai's most colorful and popular Hindu festivals such as Ganesh Chaturthi and Divali, both of which draw visitors wanting to share in such cultural exchanges. Some of the most popular attractions are those with historical connections, such as the Gateway to India, Chattrapathi Shivaji Terminus, the Prince of Wales Museum, and Elephanta Island. Elephanta Island is about an hour's boat journey across the harbor and its prime attraction is its rock-cut Hindu shrines, which date from the seventh century. The finest is a 20-foot carving of the god Shiva in three roles: as Creator, Protector, and Destroyer. East of Mumbai in Maharashtra state, the Ajanta and Ellora caves are also popular destinations and contain paintings and carvings that are among the world's finest examples of Hindu and Buddhist art.

▲ The Taj Hotel in Mumbai is one of the most exclusive in India and a favorite with tourists.

Open spaces

Despite Mumbai's extremely dense population, it is still possible to find open space. Within the city the *maidans* offer a popular respite from the hustle, but the favored escapes are along the water's edge. Marine Drive and Chowpatty Beach are particularly popular and throng in the evenings with crowds who come to enjoy the cool ocean breeze and watch some amazing sunsets. In Malabar Hill, where British administrators and merchants built large and expensive houses during the 19th century, are the Hanging Gardens, which date back to the 1880s. The landscaped gardens provide one of the best views of Mumbai, looking out toward Marine Drive and across the Arabian Sea. Farther out from the city center to the north is Sanjay Gandhi (Borivali) National Park. Covering 40 square miles of forest and hills, the park offers leopard safaris right on the edge of one of the world's largest cities! It is also known for the Kanheri Caves, a group of over 100 Buddhist caves hewn from the rock between the second and ninth centuries.

▲ August Kranti Maidan near the Chowpatty district is one of Mumbai's many open spaces, popular as an escape from the hustle and bustle of the streets.

The Mumbai environment

Urbanization, industrialization, increased traffic levels, and a still rapidly growing population combine to present Mumbai with some major environmental challenges. Air pollution, for example, is among the worst in the world and waste disposal is a major problem that has contaminated waterways and turned them into stinking open sewers. Given the emphasis on growth and the provision of basic needs, sustainability is often not a priority for Mumbaikars or city authorities.

Air quality

Industry and vehicles emit high levels of carbon monoxide, carbon dioxide, and lead into Mumbai's air. Industrial pollution is clearly evident in districts such as Kurla, Chembur, and New Mumbai, where a dirty haze often shrouds the city. Few vehicles in Mumbai are equipped with catalytic converters (which reduce emissions) and as road traffic has increased their contribution to air pollution has become enormous. BEST is testing buses that run on natural gas as a measure to reduce pollution, and the city corporation MCGM has banned rickshaws from the city center for the same reason. But such measures are minor given the scale of the problem, and the constant exposure to polluted air means 60 percent of Mumbaikars have a mild but lasting throat or nose irritation (rhinitis). During the hot and humid monsoon season, the heat-retaining properties of the asphalt and concrete, and the heat churned out by air conditioning units, exacerbate matters as the city's air becomes a sweltering cauldron of a mixture of pollutants.

Waste disposal

Mumbaikars are avid recyclers, with recycling a major industry in the city. Despite this, trash disposal is a huge problem for the corporation. Waste removal throughout much of Mumbai is highly inadequate, with no regular collections. Trash chokes streams, beaches, and areas of vacant land. Every day, the city generates 8,600 tons of trash, which is collected, transported, and dumped in landfills to the north and east. With such a huge volume of waste, city landfills fill up quickly, and then new sites

▲ A cow grazes on garbage dumped in the street in the Powai district of Mumbai. Waste is a major environmental problem for the city to deal with.

have to be found. Landfills and other developments are steadily nibbling away at coastal mangrove swamps, which are rich in plant and animal life and help protect against storm damage and erosion.

Environmentalists maintain that the MCGM's development plans threaten much of the remaining 5,065 acres of mangrove swamp and salt marsh.

▶ Cardboard collected from across the city is sorted and prepared for shipment to manufacturers for reuse or reprocessing.

CASE STUDY

Syamji Patel, waste seller

Syamji Patel, aged 45, is one of many people across Mumbai who make their living by sorting and selling trash for recycling. Waste is a major problem for Mumbai, with few formal collections. Rivers fill with trash (especially plastic bags) and turn into open sewers as they become blocked with waste. Syamji has been in the waste collection business for 25 years and explains how it works. "I pay waste collectors a small sum (around one rupee a bottle, for example) for each item of recyclable waste that they collect. I then sort it into different materials. I sell bottles to bottling plants, mainly for reuse by the breweries. Paper goes to paper mills across Maharashtra, and plastics are sold at wholesale recycling markets to industry users. People from all over Mumbai make it their business to collect anything that can be recycled. There is a saying in England that 'where there is muck there is money.' Here in Mumbai there is plenty of muck, so we make money out of recycling it!"

Flooding

Flooding is an endemic problem in low-lying parts of Mumbai during the rainy season. Drainage channels blocked by discarded waste rapidly fill up and flood during the heavy monsoon rains, and many of Mumbai's natural floodplains surrounding creeks and marshes have been developed for housing, industry, even golf courses. Such developments further undermine the ability of the city to cope with sudden downpours of rain, typical of the monsoon.

The 2005 floods

In July 2005, Mumbai made international news when a week of disastrous floods killed over 400 people. The floods occurred after ultra-heavy monsoon rains drenched the city. The floodwaters disrupted urban transportation systems, sewers and sanitation, and electricity supplies. Local creeks and particularly the Mithi River in the west burst their banks, flooding roads, railroads, and suburbs. Train services were suspended, leaving thousands stranded in flood-stricken areas. Marooned cars and buses blocked the streets, hindering emergency services. In some areas electricity supplies became unsafe.

The 2005 floods were made worse both by high tides and the failure of the city's storm drains. Designed over a century ago, these were in poor repair and blocked by trash in many areas. Designed to shut during high tides to prevent seawater swamping Mumbai, the drains backed up and actually prevented floodwater from draining away safely. With communications disrupted, the authorities were unable to issue adequate warnings to the public to evacuate the worst hit areas or to warn of dangers such as electrocution.

▲ The Mahim River, heavily polluted, was one of the major flooding areas in 2005. Many makeshift homes built along its course were flooded and hundreds of lives were lost.

▲ Slum housing encroaches into the mangrove swamps that have historically protected Mumbai from flooding. Such homes were seriously flooded in 2005 and remain at risk of any repeat of heavy floods.

Overdevelopment

Environmentalists maintain that recent development projects were also to blame, in particular the recent destruction of 1.5 square miles of coastal mangroves, to create land for new housing, landfills, and recreational facilities. The mangrove swamps act as a natural buffer in the event of flooding, absorbing water from high seas or rising rivers, and thus protecting the land. A new overpass across the mouth of the Mithi River, the Bandra-Worli Sealink, has narrowed the river estuary. This is thought to have caused the Mithi to burst its banks, making the flooding worse.

After the 2005 floods the MCGM promised a serious overhaul of its disaster management plans. It pledged to improve its early warning system for the public, including erecting electronic boards at key points in the city. New search and rescue teams were set up in flood-prone areas, while a special committee is investigating the drainage problems of the Mithi. Above all the council pledged to improve communication between branches of its huge organization, including between the police and the transportation and electricity authority, since lack of communication between these agencies is thought to have increased the death toll in 2005.

▼ The Bandra-Worli Sealink is a new bridge being constructed across Mahim Bay. Environmentalists are concerned at the impact the project could have on the local environment.

▲ Workers in the dock district fill sacks of coal by hand for use in the city. Burning coal produces emissions that add to the problems of air pollution in Mumbai.

Power

Mumbai's energy needs have risen steadily as the city's population and economy have grown. The city's power, supplied by BEST, comes from hydroelectricity, nuclear energy, and power stations burning oil and coal. In 2003, India's new Electricity Act came into force. This law requires all electricity providers in India to generate at least 10 percent of their energy from renewable sources. To meet this requirement BEST plans to use solar power to supply part of the city's lighting. It is also looking into the possibility of generating energy by burning waste—which could also help to solve the problem of garbage disposal.

▼ Lake Tudsi, in Borivali National Park, was built in the 19th century to supply water to Mumbai. The city now struggles to provide enough water.

Water and sewage

Mumbai's rising population is straining the city's water supplies. Depleted groundwater supplies (from aquifers, natural reservoirs formed by porous rocks) are causing some local wells to dry up, while others are being contaminated with seawater because the water table is low.

Sewage is treated at Bandra and Worli on the west coast, near the mouth of the Mithi River. However, the city's sewage treatment facilities are unable to deal with the volume of waste created daily and as a result much sewage enters coastal waters untreated. The same is true for industrial wastes, and so the coastal waters around Mumbai are heavily polluted.

▼ Water treatment plants provide clean water for Mumbai residents, but they are unable to keep pace with the demand of the growing population.

Milind Vibhute, water engineer

Milind Vibhute is the assistant water engineer for Mumbai and has worked for the city corporation for 18 years. Mumbai's main source of water is Modek Sagar reservoir, 60 miles to the north of the city. The water is stored in 26 service reservoirs beneath the city and distributed to users through a network of over 3,000 miles of pipes. The city is now facing major problems with water supply, as Milind explains. "The system dates from Victorian times and still works pretty well. It processes and delivers 3.1 billion liters [819 million gallons] of water a day, but the expansion of the city and its population means this is 20 percent less than the city actually needs. In 10 years' time, the increase in Mumbai's population is expected to increase the daily demand to about 7 billion liters—that's more than twice what we produce now! We are not sure where this water will come from, as the rains are already failing us in some years. Our plans to meet future needs include harvesting water from rooftops, drilling new wells to reach groundwater, and building desalination plants to use seawater."

Potential hazards

Environmentalists question the wisdom of continuing to expand Mumbai, with sea levels rising worldwide because of global warming. Even a small rise in water level could swamp the city via its storm drains within the 21st century. Much of Mumbai is extremely low-lying, just 33 to 49 feet above sea level, though to the north, Salsette Island rises to a height of 1,476 feet. Over the last 400 years land has been reclaimed from the swamps and turned over to industrial and domestic use on a piecemeal basis, with little thought for the long-term consequences.

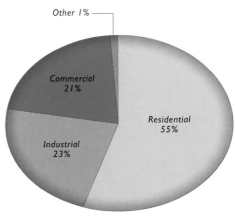

▲ Energy consumption by use (%).

The Mumbai of tomorrow

The MCGM has come up with a strategy for the city's future, based on the prediction that Mumbai will be the world's second largest city by 2020, with an estimated population of 28.5 million. However, the city's infrastructure is already groaning and further massive expansion will test it severely.

▼ New offices in the BKC district of the city are an example of the global future that city officials envisage for the Mumbai of 2020.

A future vision

By 2020 India is predicted to be the world's third largest economy after the United States and China. The MCGM has a bold vision to capitalize on this opportunity and make Mumbai "India's Shanghai"— modeled on the Chinese city renowned for its global trade. Mumbai is certainly well placed for this, with assets such as its deep water port, its low cost, and hardworking and enterprising population (a high proportion of which speaks good English, the international business language).

Jonny Joseph and the 2020 Vision

The Mumbai Taskforce for Vision 2020 is a division of MCGM with responsibility for planning the future of the city. Their main challenges include the need to resolve overcrowding in the slums, to update an infrastructure stretched to capacity, and to tackle the continual influx of new immigrants to the city. Many of the plans so far announced focus on attracting more foreign businesses, and this has attracted criticism from groups who say little is being done to alleviate the problems of Mumbai's growing poor. But the Municipal Commissioner, Jonny Joseph, explains that the pressures of globalization mean Mumbai must take these measures or risk being left behind: "My vision is to make Mumbai a first class city within my lifetime—on a par with London and New York. By considered and careful upgrading of the entire infrastructure I believe we can achieve this goal together. It will take many millions of rupees and many millions of worker-hours, but we will do it. We must!"

Overcoming the obstacles

The MCGM has numerous obstacles to overcome if it is to achieve its ambitions of Mumbai as one of the world's leading global cities. They include an overstretched infrastructure that will need improving (particularly in transportation, water, and communications) to meet the needs of foreign investors and local population alike. Such improvements must also take greater account of environmental implications, unlike recently constructed roads that actually damaged the environment, leading to erosion and the silting-up of the harbor. Most importantly, however, Mumbai must find solutions that enable more of its predominately poor population to enjoy the benefits of living in one of the world's most important cities.

There is little doubt that globalization will continue to bring economic prosperity to the city, but to what extent this is shared by the majority of Mumbai's citizens will be vital in determining the long-term sustainability of this global city.

Glossary

acetylene A colorless gas that burns with a very hot flame that can cut steel.

ascetic Austere; describes a person who practices severe self-discipline.

assign To grant or give.

autonomous Self-governing.

biodiverse Having a wide range of living species.

bureaucratic Having an organizational system that operates through rules.

caste The hereditary class system of India.

catalytic converter A device fitted to a vehicle's exhaust system to clean up the waste fumes released.

compensation An award, usually of money, paid to someone in recognition that a wrong has been done.

converge To meet.

dowry Goods or money paid on marriage to the husband by the bride's family.

ethnic Having to do with large groups of people who share a common language, culture, nationality, religion, or racial origin.

exuberantly Extravagantly, with relish.

frenetic Frenzied.

global warming Rising temperatures worldwide, caused by the increase of carbon dioxide and other gases in the atmosphere that trap the Sun's heat.

groundwater Natural stores of water contained in porous (sponge-like) rocks underground.

industrialize To develop from an economy based on the manual labor of individuals or small groups to one based on large-scale, mechanized industries and manufacturing.

informal sector Businesses that are not officially registered and so avoid paying taxes and complying with regulations such as wage and safety laws.

infrastructure The basic facilities needed for a country to function, including electricity, communications, and transportation.

inflation A general increase in prices within a country.

Jain An adherent of Jainism. Jains believe in salvation by reaching perfection through a succession of lifetimes, and they practice respect for all living creatures.

landfill A pit in the ground where trash is buried.

lucrative Profitable.

merchandise Goods that are for sale.

nutrition Nourishment; food.

Parsi An Indian adherent of the Zoroastrian religion.

partition On India's Independence in 1947, the division of the subcontinent into Hindu-dominated India and Muslim-dominated Pakistan.

reclaimed land Land converted for housing or for growing crops, such as by draining swamps.

renewable energy Energy that comes from sources that will not run out, such as the Sun, wind, and flowing water.

sewage Dirty water from homes and factories, containing chemicals and human waste.

Sikhism A monotheistic religion founded in the Punjab (now in modern India and Pakistan) in the 15th century. Adherents, called Sikhs, reject the caste system.

recycling The process of reclaiming useful materials from waste so that they can be used again.

taboo Something that is forbidden by society.

Zoroastrianism A monotheistic religion founded in what is now Iran before the coming of Islam. Adherents are required to perform good deeds.

Further information

Useful Web sites:

Bombay First
http://www.bombayfirst.org/
Statistics, economic information, and other facts about doing business in Mumbai.

Homeless International
http://www.homeless-international.org
The Web site of a charity that helps communities in poor areas, including Mumbai, build housing and infrastructure.

The Mumbai Pages
http://theory.tifr.res.in/bombay/
Up-to-date information on the city's architecture, people, food, history, leisure activities, and more.

"Mumbai's Looming Ecological Disaster"
http://news.bbc.co.uk/2/hi/south_asia/4737153.stm
A BBC News article on Mumbai's worsening environmental hazards.

Books:

Allaby, Michael. *Countries of the World: India.* New York: Facts On File, 2005. A highly illustrated introduction to the country as a whole, including Mumbai, for readers grade 6 and up.

Desai, Anita. *The Village by the Sea.* London: Heinemann, 1982. A novel about Hari, a boy from a coastal village in India who runs away to Mumbai. He hopes to find the glamorous city that everyone talks about but instead finds a life of poverty and endless slums.

Monga, Sunjoy. *City Forest: Mumbai's National Park.* Mumbai: India Book House, 2000. A photographic tour of the amazing biodiversity in the heart of Mumbai.

Time Out: Mumbai. London: Time Out Guides, 2006. A comprehensive travel guide to Mumbai.

Vakil, Ardashir. *Beach Boy.* New York: Scribner, 1998. A coming-of-age novel about Cyrus, a Mumbai boy, as he deals with family struggles and encounters food, films, school, and girls.

Index